Another Place Altogether

Another Place Altogether

Poems by

Candice M. Kelsey

© 2025 Candice M. Kelsey. All rights reserved.
This material may not be reproduced in any form, published,
reprinted, recorded, performed, broadcast,
rewritten or redistributed without
the explicit permission of Candice M. Kelsey.
All such actions are strictly prohibited by law.

Cover design by Shay Culligan
Cover image by Jayson Boesman on Unsplash
Author photo by Israel M. Kelsey

ISBN: 978-1-63980-998-1

Kelsay Books
502 South 1040 East, A-119
American Fork, Utah 84003
Kelsaybooks.com

for Los Angeles and Augusta

Acknowledgments

Thank you to the following publications, in which versions of these poems previously appeared:

About Place Journal: "Ludicrous Optimism Pantoum"
Anacapa Review: "Ode to a Bartender at the Charlotte Douglas Airport, Terminal A"
Anti-Heroin Chic: "Meditation on Selective Memory Begins with Jimmy Carter," "Candice"
Assaracus Journal of Gay Poetry: "The Birth of President Donald Trump, c. 2016"
Barstow and Grand: "Sonnet Where Rhyme and Meter Fail the Poem Like Capitalism Fails the Child"
Bicoastal Review: "Menopause: A Cento from Female Poets Laureate"
The Blue Mountain Review: "[C]ars Poetica"
Connecticut River Review: "Flesh and Bone"
The Cove Magazine: "American Tragedy"
DSTL Arts: "L.A.'s Bitch," "A Tale of Two Cities"
Emerge Literary Journal: "Freedom," "Photosynthesis Reversed"
The Fourth River: "Summer and Its Humidity"
Gone Lawn: "Strange Creature," "Balish"
Gyroscope Review: "L.A. Nocturne"
Hole in the Head Review: "Ekphrastic; on Anxiety, My Golden-Caped Lover," "For My Daughter on Her 21st Birthday," "Because Your Husband's Shirt is Ironed," "Back in Los Angeles," "A Tree Falls in the Forest of Men"
The Hooghly Review: "To My Step Father-in-Law," "Cool"
Hudson Valley Writers Guild: "Daddy, I'm Fine"
Libre: "Sonnet XIV"
Lines + Stars: "Meditation on Parenting"
Loblolly Press: "I See Fallen Trees"
Lobster Salad & Champagne: "At a Local Wine Tasting, I Consider Divorce"

Miracle Monocle: "This Tender Dwelling"
Moonstone Arts Center: "To Be a Word in a Poem"
Moss Puppy Mag: "Resolution"
Muleskinner Journal: "Parable with Flags, Humidity & Loss"
North Dakota Quarterly: "Dr. Blasey Ford Explained, 'Indelible in the Hippocampus is the Laughter,' and I Can't Forget It"
Olney Magazine: "Tonight, My Friend Shows Me How to Give Myself a Hug"
Orca Literary Journal: "Plastic Orange Lei"
Passengers Journal: "Ode to Ms. Pac-Man"
Poets Reading the News: "May Day, May Day"
Porcupine Literary: "Yes, It Could"
Press 53's Prime Number: "To Be the Vowel in an Abjad Family"
River & South Review: "Mothers & Daughters"
River Heron Review: "Chronic Prepositions"
Roi Fainéant Press: "The Death of Lowly Worm"
Sheila-Na-Gig: "Experts Say Reciting the Alphabet Backwards Helps Manage Stress"
SoFloPoJo: "I Knew a Father," "Ecstatic Ghosts"
Sonora Review: "SELF Portrait as Character List," "Playing Hide 'n Seek with My Father's Ghost"
Stone Circle Review: "Re-Reading *Beowulf,* I Remember My Mother's Address Book"
Sunday Mornings at the River: "Ekphrastic; on a Lover's Betrayal"
Thimble Lit Mag: "Not for the Faint of Heart"
Tiny Seed Literary Journal: "What Never Seems to Happen"
Troublemaker Firestarter: "Family Fun and Sparklers for the Kiddos"
Wild Roof Journal: "Into the Womb of Air"
Writer's Digest: "Full Self-Driving"

Gratitude

I'll begin with my children. Thank you, Georgia Rae, Mikey, and Israel. I feel it every day and never tire of saying it—I am so lucky to be your mother. You are my beginning, my ending, and everything in between. To the great people at Kelsay Books, Karen, Olivia, and Jenna, thank you for believing in this project! You've brought my words to life with such care and expertise. Oodles of gratitude to Ann Wagner, Dhana Musil, Dzvinia Orlowsky, and Luanne Castle, my loyal and brilliant writer friends who never ignore my endless questions or say no to looking at drafts of poems, no matter how dreadful. Your generosity and wisdom astound me. To Fawn and Colleen, my support system in Los Angeles, thank you for welcoming me home with pastries, bookstores, bike rides, and picnics. To Laurie, for being there always. To Perseus, Hawk, Bryce, Dolly, Winston, Orbit, Sam, Elaine, and Yonah, much appreciation for the countless moments of playful distraction. To Sav and Iris, gratitude for the music recommendations, unhinged texts, and delightful hi-jinks.

Hats off to the writers who have inspired me over the past few years, and whose fingerprints are found both subtly and overtly in this collection: Kurt Brown, Ocean Vuong, Annie Dillard, C.K. Williams, Theodore Roethke, Charlotte Perkins Gilman, Louise Erdrich, Mary Shelley, Louise Bogan, Jericho Brown, Terrance Hayes, Chen Chen, Ilya Kaminsky, Eavan Boland, Carolyn Forché, Kay Ryan, Seamus Heaney, Jose Hernandez Diaz, Sharon Olds, James Wright, Lucille Clifton, Matsuo Bashō, Charles Simic, Margaret Fuller, Josephine Jacobsen, Maxine Kumin, Rita Dove, Natasha Trethewey, Tracy K. Smith, Joy Harjo, Ada Limón, Ellen Bass, and Mary Oliver.

I'll end with my YULA community. Thank you Shterny, Diana, Maya, Victoria, Chelsea, Stephen, Bill, Fletch, Alex M., Allegra, Rivkah, Yehudis, Doc, Mindy, Racheli, Shandalov, Orit, Shira, Gabby, Ziva, and the whole staff; working with you is an honor. I stand in awe of your passion for students, love of life, and indefatigable sense of humor. But most of all, I am grateful for your acceptance of me. And of course, thank you to the remarkable young women who inspire me daily—my students.

Contents

ENDINGS

L.A. Nocturne	21
Resolution	23
Experts Say Reciting the Alphabet Backwards Helps Manage Stress	25
L.A.'s Bitch	26
Thanks God	27
Ekphrastic; on a Lover's Betrayal	29
A List of Curses	30
Ekphrastic; on Anxiety, My Golden-Caped Lover	32
A Tree Falls in the Forest of Men	33
Library Holds List of the Dead	34
For My Daughter on Her 21st Birthday	36
Ode to Ms. Pac-Man	38
The Birth of President Donald Trump, c. 2016	41
Jacaranda Tree	42
I Knew a Father	43
Daddy, I'm Fine	44
Freedom	47
Dr. Blasey Ford Explained, "Indelible in the Hippocampus is the Laughter," and I Can't Forget It	48
Strange Creature	50
Duplex for Your Former Principal Who, Like Your Mother, Is a Gemini	51
Leaving a Legacy	52
Balish	56
To Be the Vowel in an Abjad Family	57
In Response to *The Atlantic*'s "Elite College Students Who Can't Read Books," October 1, 2024	60

Sonnet Where Rhyme and Meter Fail the Poem Like Capitalism Fails the Child	61
To My Step Father-in-Law	62
What She Learns	63
Sonnet XIV	65
Meditation on Parenting	66
What Never Seems to Happen	67
To Be a Word in a Poem	68
Cold-blooded	71
Re-Reading *Beowulf,* I Remember My Mother's Address Book	72
Hunger	74
Meditation on Selective Memory Begins with Jimmy Carter	76
SELF Portrait as Character List	78
American Tragedy	79
Golden Trowel; Cross Country Move, L.A. to Georgia	80

BEGINNINGS

Parable with Flags, Humidity & Loss	83
Candice	84
Tonight, My Friend Shows Me How to Give Myself a Hug	86
The Art of Encouragement	88
A Gift	90
Cool	92
Flesh and Bone	94
Because Your Husband's Shirt is Ironed	96

On Democracy	98
I See Fallen Trees	100
Into the Womb of Air	102
Mothers & Daughters	103
Photosynthesis Reversed	105
Playing Hide 'n Seek with My Father's Ghost	106
Family Fun and Sparklers for the Kiddos	108
Chronic Prepositions	109
Renewable Energy	110
Full Self-Driving	112
[C]ars Poetica	114
Not for the Faint of Heart	116
A Tale of Two Cities; or, Alerts from Citizen App While I Commute	118
To the Bros in My Row	119
Yes, It Could	121
Back in Los Angeles	122
To Which a Celebration of Life	124
Epiphany After Missing Your Connecting Flight to Augusta Airport	125
At a Local Wine Tasting, I Consider Divorce	126
Dear Potential Lover, Don't Bother	127
Ecstatic Ghosts	128
A Mother Commutes from Georgia to L.A. for a Higher Paying Job	130
Summer with Its Humidity	132
Plastic Orange Lei	133
The Death of Lowly Worm	135
Ludicrous Optimism Pantoum	137
Ode to a Bartender at the Charlotte Douglas Airport, Terminal A	139

Menopause: A Cento from Female Poets Laureate	142
Ghazal Where I Learn to Love Myself	144
May Day, May Day	146
Chimneys and Buddhas	147
Fist Pump	149
This Tender Dwelling	150

Praise

With a striking and unforgettable voice, poet Candice M. Kelsey's words will echo well beyond these pages. At its core, *Another Place Altogether* wrestles with what it means to be "An only daughter [who] is the truthteller, down / like a family wound, wounded and unwound." This formally expansive collection asks, "who can reach across the seas of mother and daughter?" These poems are an act of reclamation, in which the speaker learns self-compassion: "how to love, / not to kill."

Bethany Jarmul
Author of *Lightning Is a Mother*

Another Place Altogether probes the delicate often painful bonds within families. From the present to the past, from Augusta, GA to Los Angeles, no relationship is left unexplored in poems of candor, power, and emotion. Beginning at the end, Kelsey invokes the need for "reparenting," noting that "Adulthood requires an untiling." A grandmother leaves "a legacy of disordered eating," and a mother's degenerative arthritis is "a mouse climbing through me / his tiny knapsack full / of time location & motion." Kelsey eleoquently concludes by noting the importance of self-compassion, if not self-forgiveness, and most imporantly, "How to stay."

David Cazden
Author of *New Stars and Constellations*

ENDINGS

The animals know: their ancient, invisible trails cross
and re-cross our own like scars that have healed long ago.
Their country is not our country but another place altogether.

—Kurt Brown, "Road Trip"

L.A. Nocturne

The week ended today,
the week that would never end.

Saturday is on the branch,
distant outline of a bird
or delicate soul.

Sunday is damselfly promise,
its nymphal wing flutter
filmy and net-veined.

Seven o'clock sundown,
Children sprawl and splash
in the neighbor's pool.

I hear my street's construction
stop, hold its tongue;

familiar-voiced laborers quiet
hammers and saws. Slam
pick-up truck doors,

stress and windows down,
crank up Mega 96.3 KXOL—

Scents dance from ovens;
apartment 4B's challah, braided
and baked, is cooling.

Under the sunset's shawl
I listen to the Dodgers
on iHeart radio; Ohtani aims
toward our shared ether.

The desire to improve myself
at night disturbs me.

It is the weekend
as it had been last weekend.
I am both rider and horse;

today I can do what I like.

Saturday hops down the branch,
its wings volant, its beak
full of damselflies.

Resolution

Only the future revisits the past.
  —Ocean Vuong

Today, she attempts reparenting herself, starts
with her parents' table
long ago sealed and grouted
       with mosaic tiles.

Leather gloves and hammer, ready to catch shards
of a childhood. The strength
of a promise
           to finally get healthy.

Adulthood requires an untiling. Slow
acceptance of self as table,
the chaos of voices,
              silent scrape of chairs.

This familiar kitchen surface, cliché
ceramic ocean scene
of amber, aqua, and indigo squares
                 cresting like memory.

She taps each tile, scrapes the pattern
with patience. Fifty years
of shame, self-sabotage, and fear of intimacy
                 like garlic's tunic

peeling papery relics. Anything can be fixed. Even
under Pharaoh's rule.
           Deft hands, the hope

of a grown child floating alone, can
make a life. Beautiful
covenants begin
         with destruction.

Experts Say Reciting the Alphabet Backwards Helps Manage Stress

Zucchini rots from small bruises on the blossom, much as
your hands budded plum from piling firewood into the Durango.
Ximeno Avenue and a Los Angeles sky, we wanted a fire
where once we wanted nothing but each other; no one
Van Morrisoned like us in bed, like two seeds planted. I can't
usher squash, corn, or pole beans from Georgia red clay
today—intentions fail. And Augusta's fall line creates two
soil zones. You collected so much kindling then, felt no
reason to leave dried twigs and branches in the underbrush;
quiet as a vine borer you delivered boughs to our front
porch. Logs you rolled from felled trees, limbed and bucked,
obstructed the hallway of our mid-modern century. Life
never promised the right size hearth. You stoked the embers
morning and night, obsessing over the flue and poker—
losing the point of warmth. Here we find our fall line. Feral
kittens birthed in our bed, and now you sleep on the closet floor
just to be near the litter, silent as ash. You like to collect.
I cannot be an accumulation, will not play your compilation
hoarding into the mystic. We are Piedmont and Coastal
geography run through by a Mesozoic shoreline of oblique-slip
faults. Before leaving you, I planted winter vegetable seeds,
explained that squash, corn, and beans are called *the three sisters:*
determined to nurture each other in the soil like family. Are
cold sticks and seeds the final blossom, the end of a marriage
broken like twenty years of rot? We prune, find tiny bruises.
Ask too much of language with our endings, beginnings.

L.A.'s Bitch

My 75-pound boxer enjoys jumping into my lap any chance she gets. If anyone gets in her way, she nuzzles her head between them and me. Sometimes she throws a hip check and celebrates small victories by resting head and front paws on my legs. Exaggerated exhales and moments later a fabricated yawn adds flare to her conquest. I feel loved, even favored for a minute or two before I get up and tend to the whiskerless dry nose of my day, where I jump into the lap of this city, nuzzling again and again between the shoulders of an angel. I want it to scratch my ears, pat my haunches, and sit for longer than ten minutes. Day after day I am the bad dog begging for approval. Sent to the back yard, stuffed into a crate while Los Angeles pulses down the freeway doing what it does with people who matter. Fate releases a hyperbolic sigh, yawns for spite. Still, I jump for keys at the door.

Thanks God

she tells me, this Argentinian
surprise of a woman seated by me
at a bridal shower so proud
that she and her husband,
who once trained Perón's horses,
thanks God paid off their home
and now, *aleluya,* can retire
free of worry, *thanks God yes.*

I too thank God I am here
like the smooth stones holding
a gossamer tablecloth where we
enjoy sandwiches de miga.
Thanks God I am just a guest
like the faded storybooks stacked
to hold succulent DIY centerpieces,
thick and hardy. I sip a maté

relieved not to be the bride's
slender twin in a dress too lowcut
for abuela's approval. Thanks
God I am but a decoration in linen
at this West L.A. garden party
rather than a spotted military horse
broken by a dictator for parades.
Today I am nothing. But

my hands are double-doors
greeting each new tablemate.
How do you know the bride-to-be?
My eyes become the Malbec

gleam of polite conversation, thanks
God, between adivina el anillo
and the bouquet of gift ribbons.
My laugh releases into air

like the strings of a charango,
soon forgotten inside my shell,
thanks God. Life has not broken me
after all. For I too am proud
to have paid off anxiety's mortgage,
aleluya. I move through parties
without worry, content and free
as any long-forgotten horse.

Ekphrastic; on a Lover's Betrayal

while viewing Magritte's "The Menaced Assassin"

You stabbed & stabbed.
I saw your work—you,
like Magritte's voyeur, his
menaced assassin.
Why did you peer through
the window from
behind the neighbor's fence?
Enter the room,
useless coward with a knife. See
the victim on the table,
moon-pale and still.

Unruly lover,
I sank my fingers
into the gore & tore that
shit wide open,
shredding muscle, exposing bone.
Could you hear
the irreparable pops & hisses
through your glasses?

I kissed my bloody fingers
then pillowed what
breath was left
in the lungs of our love.
Detectives in bowler
hats waited, with net & club, they
waited to find
what had been exposed—
a stupid corpse of us.
I can be brutal too. Finish
whatever you start.

A List of Curses

to condemn hands that muzzle the night.
Condemn the Late Show with its laugh track,
Glowing across a father's face on his daughter's neck.
Condemn a brother with binoculars by his window,
Condemn frat boys chugging bunk-bed conquests,
A bubble off plumb, a distant bubble off spirit level
Like deer hit across highways, inside the heart of a girl.

Condemn the scent of a Beverly Hills exam room
With state-of-the-art ultrasounds, the tick of a fetal clock
Under the pillow of placenta midday, then the pelvic.
Condemn the extended and meaningless small talk
Of latexed hands resting on your breast, exposed.
Condemn his extra stitch to *make you a virgin again*,
And years later condemn the ghost-fingers fluttering inside.

Condemn the hunting of sea birds and loggerhead turtles
And the carbon and plastic of habitat destruction
And bait and offal of long lines and gillnets
Entangling bycatch in the Baltic beyond the harbor.
Free Paul Watson, and condemn Japanese factory ships
With drones and explosive-tipped harpoons,
Singing Antarctic dirges while cutting into blue whales.

Condemn the clicking heels of doom down hallways.
Condemn principals who corner their teachers,
Condemn the 4:15 closed door after everyone has left,
The hands, the wet mouthed assaults that never stop.
When the giant water bug injects poison into the frog,
And no one believes it, we know the teacher must resign.
Like Annie Dillard described, the innards liquefy.

Condemn Evangelical pastors, Sunday jackals.
Week after week comparing our girl bodies to Oreos,
Passed from hand to hand, cookies no one wants to eat.
Scotch tape *sluts* losing stick, picking up lint, hair and dirt.
Bodies round as lollipops used up, too many licks.
Condemn purity culture with this spirit level, half a bubble
Off plumb, and with the songs of a thousand Cassandras.

Ekphrastic; on Anxiety, My Golden-Caped Lover

while viewing Klimt's "The Kiss"

If art is a line around our thoughts as Gustav Klimt declared,
Then what does that mean for my depression & anxiety

Which are nothing if not a heap, or a thrust, of lines?

Can I knot them, know them, sever, belay or betray them—
Are they coiled too tightly? If art can be a simple geometric

Concept, I wonder what that means for mental health.

Do its lines hug like a Mobius strip, or twist its neck around
A galvanized dock cleat, or string the eaves like holiday lights?

When the glow on the lake signals the sun to call it a day,

Can we motor in toward the dock & toss its lines over
Like C.K. Williams tossed his lines across the page, tongue

Like the lovers in Klimt's golden mosaic? Self-negativity
& intrusive thoughts like recurring motifs, geometric,

Our consciousness an obscene embrace called poetry.

A Tree Falls in the Forest of Men

1992 will leave you worse for wear | you will train for your first triathlon | days will be spent cycling, running, purging | watching *Silence of the Lambs* in the Oxford Theater will undo you | the scene when she helps him load furniture into his van | this will be the year you break your middle finger helping a stranger untangle the leashes of five dogs from a tree | you will apply to law school & cram eighteen final credits to graduate & ask your professor to stop calling | your parents finally divorce | your father will refuse to remove his wedding ring | your mother will start an over-fifty singles group at Good Shepherd Church—*Betwixters* | a *fuck you* thirty years in the making | your father a lamb to the slaughter | takes in feral cats | places a felled Sycamore tree in his living room just for them | when they chase each other the branches shake as if the soul of the tree | this will be the year loneliness wins | the silence of bark | you will live at home after graduation | intern at a firm downtown | fall in love in the file room | your lover will get *Miss Saigon* tickets to celebrate your law school acceptance | that night your older brother will say *this guy is a loser* | you are forbidden to go | stupid you don't answer the door | your brother will not remember this night | your lover will leave in his old Chevette | you will make a mixtape of break-up songs | in your recurring dream the felled Sycamore sprouts wings | you are heard

Library Holds List of the Dead

Glowing in digital obscurity as a corpse flower
whose bloom emerges every seven years,

thick stem of energy then stench and decay.
Something more valuable than a story remains

where the dead once searched by author or title,
no longer select a location and wait to be notified.

I squeeze my eyes shut. Listen to the susurrus
of names pouring interests like ancient libations:

Bluegrass: A History, hold expired. *Prague: A Guide
to Viewing Art in the City of a Hundred Spires*,

late fee $3.90. The record of a life spent reading,
a hidden register no one signs. The unremembered

speak in dog-eared pages. From the return bin
at a local branch, tiny monument to its patrons,

comes the space between pages. All book drops
a bloom of silent returns and pebbled dirge.

The holds shelf too portends each book's fate,
its alphabetical spines and paper tongues mark

time like eager spring bulbs in sandy loam. *Dunn,
Robinson,* and *Steinborn* don't come. Borrowing

a book is to breach the threshold of possibility.
The dead glow, know life cannot be owned.

For My Daughter on Her 21ˢᵗ Birthday

November 2023

It's a girl! You sparked six pounds
six ounces measuring nineteen
inches with blood-red lips.

Four months after you were born
to our shock and awe
Baghdad fell from a U.S. bombing
campaign and you took
my nipple as Saddam Hussein's
Ba'athist regime toppled:

*We are ready to sacrifice our souls
so as not to give up Iraq,*
Hussein said, *so no one will think
America is capable of breaking Iraqis.*

The month you were conceived
President Bush
declared Iraq one part of
the Evil Axis as our bodies
created yours and war
prepared a million fatalities:

*America will not permit the world's
most dangerous regimes
to threaten us with the world's
most destructive weapons.*

Two years into college
you found your voice and quit
the track team, knowing it was time

to become authentic
you shocked your father
but I was in awe.

A year before we married
in shock and awe
your father and I stood
over a hundred stories high
on the South Tower
in love on Top of the World.

If we learn nothing else from this
tragedy we learn that life
is short and there is no time for hate
—wife of Flight 93 pilot, 2002.

Tonight you turn twenty-one
and I am toppled
from shock and awe at Gaza
and Ukraine Daughter
you are living proof of
just how damn easy it is to love.

Ode to Ms. Pac-Man

She's as close to self-erasure
as humans come. Both earthbound
& profound like the process
of becoming a parent
which shatters so many parts.
Like a maze arcade video game

we are centuries of women
levitating down corridors
of hospitals in labor
dangerously close to death's
tight corners & babies
joy sticked through birth
canals marking a series
of endings & remarkable beginnings.

*Why is no woman's labor
as famous as the death of Socrates*
asks Louise Erdrich
in her memoir *The Blue Jay's Dance.*
A strong philosopher
selflessly holding forth
with one glass of hemlock
hardly compares
to the contracting of 1,000 uteruses.

Each quarter in the slot
brings transformation or trauma
like when I was ten
& for Halloween I was a salad
wearing a green polyester

bodysuit. I became
a bed of lettuce drizzled & dressed
looking fresh with clusters
of sculpted croutons. Cute game
of cherry tomatoes

& half a hard-boiled egg,
I had become
what my mother wanted:
if I could be the salad
then I could choose the salad
& if I ate the salad
then I would not be *fat*
a girl out knocking on doors
for Snickers bars & Jolly
Ranchers, my carrot

basket filling from each house.
Did Ms. Pac-man
also have a mother watching
as she rushed to eat
the fruits in her path? My
mother was a ghost
whose semi-random movements
sent me down warp-tunnels
to escape the scolding
& find a way out of her canal
or die swooning. Original
Pac-Man would fold
into himself rather than faint.

At nineteen I folded
driving the maze of I-275
& State Route 27 from Cincinnati
to Miami University
when the truck of men to my right
honked for my attention
then flashed me
their own joysticks firmly
gripped like my toes
in the stirrups & my hips quivering
open to the fruit
I needed to push out—
my daughter who refuses to wear
that fucking red bow.

The Birth of President Donald Trump, c. 2016

after Mary Shelley

By the hazy glistening light of the November moon
as it crept inside, stumbling a bit
and tearing the curtains, I beheld the ugliest, animated mess
of discolored flesh—a wretched monster
whom this nation had created.
He sat down, straightened his silk tie, and pointed
toward me with a corpse-finger.
His mouth was moving, a malevolent grin
uttering folderol of bloat and gloat
like shifting alpine glaciers.
Perhaps he meant to thank us; I do not know,
but one of his eyes was fixed
on his own reflection in the window.
He seemed detained by his own existence,
and as I rushed out the front door to escape, I saw
the echo of fiery torches and heard
the neighbors spark, *It's an early Christmas!*

Jacaranda Tree

Purple-blue trumpet,
Pier Avenue's own Gabriel,
blows indigo tears
across sidewalks our
sticky carpeting
of grief. Holy tattoos
like a hip-flesh bruise
announce mortality
though we try to see bloom
rather than doom. Its
funeral shroud foliage
unfolds. Front yard jacaranda,
periwinkle detonation,
ram's horn alarm
and Thessalonian call, lifts
its arms to clasp ours
in this spring canopy
of unavoidable mourning.

I Knew a Father

after Samuel Ace

I knew a father who was a son who was a brother who was an orphan who married a woman who was a daughter who was a sister who wanted a daughter who was not me the only sister

who knew a mother who preferred a daughter with longer hair or a daughter who liked dresses who didn't cut pretty dolls' hair who didn't draw haunted houses where ghouls demanded sandwiches where ghosts did chest presses who read *Arnold's Bodybuilding for Men* who had free reign over the girl who hid in the linen closet who lived like a punching bag like a receptacle

like a girl who knew a father who threw her into the porcelain umbrella stand who used a bamboo walking stick to make his point who left the girl who was me with skin like a forest floor like a pattern of black rain frogs

coldness knew (a mother who hated) her mother who hated her daughter who preferred cleaning her plate and asking for seconds but played by the rules of dieting games for a mother who moved the goal posts who punted the ephedrine pills who tallied the calories for a daughter

who needed protection who knew a father who found her on the couch with a boy she knew a father whose breath was whiskey whose eyes were distant who slapped her face

(who pinned me to the carpet like a girl who would never tell)

Daddy, I'm Fine

after Sinéad O'Connor

I have not done me
well
      you found the ipecac
      sorry to be   disappointing
I was a picture   torn
not your little girl
      locked in early morning shame   Jesus
      Mary and Joseph's inside-out   girl
with my hair tied back and my gray
      cotton sweats
      hands hungry for yours to squeeze
      three times: I. Love. You.
      during Mass
No I didn't do me
well
      family therapy at the EDU
      I wanted you
      to know   I could
not do
anymore Daddy
      you were bounce a quarter on my bed
      I was loose   unmade
      sleeves inverted
      neck holes   wide   pants legs
twisted sock
caught
      lint trap felt skirt   too short
      in Velcro call to boys
      I get sexy

with my hair tied back and my gray
      cotton sweats
      hands hungry for yours to squeeze
      three times: Who. Am. I.
      during Mass
frenetic you
tried to fold
      unmatched corners—too
      sensitive feeling
      real hot
      I was a picture   torn
      strong independent woman
not your little girl
Daddy my monarch my king
      I believed you
      wanted me to numb   be neat
      run to jump   into your arms
      5:00 arrivals
      make you feel   alright
but I was too
useless unlocked
      right-side-out girl
      I do what I like for fun
with my hair tied back and my gray
      cotton sweats
      just fucking hungry
      squeezing: I. Hate. You.
      into pants

Asshole I'm Fine
        locked in   the bathroom
        underneath the lights
        real cool
you caught me
        horizontal with T___
        on the green floral couch
        Jesus   Mary   Joseph
        Whore is what you wanted
Daddy
who is the real enemy
        I loved
        you

Freedom

a golden shovel after Louise Bogan's "The Dream"

Oh Lover, in the memory the toxic cane toad began
To invade Australia, and secrete his bufotoxins in blows,
Confusion kept for ninety years inflating his belly like a mane,
And shame equally old, or nearly, spreading a chytrid fungus
                                                   through his nose.

An adolescent ambushed, I fell and froze on the ground
When my dog's warm muzzle appeared, haunches
                                                   established her reign.
Sister bitch, as I lay in the daze of girlhood's shared wound,
Growled at my abuser, gnawed his hands like leather and chain.

Give me, Lover says, *specific emotions,* her tenderness a charm.
Share, she pleads, some small detail you alone claim.
Hell no, I whisper, *for he lays 30,000 eggs twice a year;*
                                            this man is out for harm,
And whether I tell it or not, it is all the same.

But, like a toad-culling robot, when I admit my father's hand
                                                        like a glove
That night slapped my sweating, my cold young cheek,
The toxic cane toad, that no conservationist can tolerate,
Leaves Northern Queensland. Native species and I
                                                     now thrive in love.

Dr. Blasey Ford Explained, "Indelible in the Hippocampus is the Laughter," and I Can't Forget It

Ishmael
was cast out

in some wood, beyond
the reach
of God's voice,
trembling.

A rustling.
And God's robe fell
silent. Cowards
always are.

But the cool air
was witness.
Ishmael's new robe,
Hagar's hair:

tangled and bitter
like the mouth
of a girl
muzzled by hands.

Always
a holding down.
The simple truth,
the swoop

of a golden eagle.
The goat caught,
tossed
off crags into

a bottomless gorge
of accusation,
denial.
Confirmation

the powerful remain
on top, laugh.

Strange Creature

A woman invited her newly widowed mother for a long visit, once things settled down. Her mother inquired if the woman still had that corn snake as a pet. When the woman sent a picture of the snake to her mother, she was sure the mother would see the snake safely behind glass, not threatening. Her mother told her snakes are evil, that they are from the devil. She also told her it was cruel to keep one in a cage. The woman asked if she would please come stay with her for a few weeks now that her mother would be alone. Her mother refused because of the *stupid snake,* but she would mail the American flag from her father's funeral as a keepsake. The woman prepared a triangular shadow frame to display the flag safely behind glass. When the box from her mother arrived, the woman found the flag, the shell casings from the military honors, and two books about the cruelty of keeping a snake.

Duplex for Your Former Principal Who, Like Your Mother, Is a Gemini

After an unwanted kiss, the telling
May cleanse years of spit from your face.

    Decades of complex PTSD soak your skin:
    You retire scarred after twenty-five years teaching.

After thirty-five years, your principal steps down, just fine;
She was two-faced, petty, and abusive. Mean as your mother.

    Your narcissistic June mother spits criticisms
    Like kisses. A Cancer, you're smudged

By disordered eating. Your conscience nudges, *we need*
To deal with the trauma. Your moon-mouth puckers.

    Fuck the drama of open-mouthed intrusions.
    You trace the stars, shell intrusive thoughts:

The intrusive face of your former boss. Open your claws.
Even the telling can't remove an unwanted kiss.

Leaving a Legacy

Grandmother,
where would we be now
if you had just held your tongue
those times your fingers pinched fat
and your mother's judgment screamed
get yourself on a diet
from inside your flesh for the crush
of my mother's worth?

Where would we be
if you had wholly accepted
whatever new shapes manifested
from my mother's adolescent thighs,
whatever terror you felt or found
from whatever size of pants
or measuring tape to waist?

You left a legacy of disordered eating
burned across her sense of self,
of tense family dinner monitoring,
its lightheaded spin of unspoken hunger.

I know I've done the hard inner work,
that my words would never
cut the bitter blade of our mouths
across my daughters' bodies.

Grandmother,
I wish you had the freedom
of weightlessness, of heaviness,
of eyes away from mirrors.

I wish you had taught my mother
        the indifference of 10
        or 20
        or 100 more pounds.
had allowed my mother to eat what she wanted
        in peace,
        or without guilt
        or after 8pm
        or not in secret
        or despite your disgust
        as you chose to hold your tongue,
had simple acceptance
when you felt your disapproval
flooding into my mother's hips,
had the strength of resolve
when you felt society's sting
in your eyes on the bloom of her curves,

and prevented the wilting of a mother-daughter relationship.

That you had made more biscuits,
served more casseroles,
threw out every bathroom scale,
        every urge to compare,
        a minute on the lips
        if you can pinch an inch,

or just smiled and put your arms around her
instead of splicing *fat* to her flesh.

I wish you had a therapist once a week,
or twice, or every day
encouraging you to stop the cycle,
to remember what a mother can lose
by spitting fat phobic language:
trust, connection, daily calls and visits,
a relationship, freedom, freedom
from the label *shitty mother,*

had the words to say
you are beautiful just the way you are,
had the foresight
when you were about to shame my mother,
had the space to accept your own body,
before birthing seven daughters,
but especially after.

Grandmother,
I wish you had almost anything else in the world
than me, standing over your memory
years since you've passed, hearing my mother's voice
burning in my head.

But here we are, flesh of our flesh,
bone of our bone, and the only gift I can give you
is that I've run from your flesh in my flesh,
broken your bone in my bone

when your words filled my mother's mouth. I've tried
to erase the parts of you that took me
so close to erasing myself.

Mother,
where would we be now
if you had been protected from her,
had ignored your mother's insults,
had loved your body—

what if I weren't ricocheting
from anorexia to bulimia,
      outpatient to inpatient,
          low-contact to no-contact with you,
stumbling through years
over broken glass
to find a path of healing and what I wish I could share—

I understand you,
love your body, my daughters' bodies, even your mother's.
    I love even the body of this world,
                which started it all.

Balish

Once, a family shared a common name and a common tongue, but to keep them safe from outsiders, the father recorded their language and hid it away inside a cave. A young girl, who had heard stories of the days when the family lived in harmony, went in search of the language. As she hiked down toward the beach looking for the mouth of the cave, she called her mother to guide her, but her mother couldn't understand her. Next, she texted her brother for help, but her brother couldn't understand her either. Language had become useless. Finally, a wise deer showed her the way to the cave, where she begged for the language to be returned. The cave told her this was impossible, but shared one word with her, and afterwards the young girl was the happiest member of the entire family, for she knew she had tried to honor the Balish name.

To Be the Vowel in an Abjad Family

is like being a trombone among tubas,
trumpets, cornets, and French horns.
The only daughter, a rebel like exiled vowels
in a consonantal family.

Today I rhythm down to curious
learning the French word for paperclip. Like
one found in the faculty lounge, pulled
from a Staples box, flimsy cardboard coffin
to be forgotten, *Le Trombone* in red.

A child is like a trombone, an instrument
without valves flapping open and shut. The one
member of a brass family using metal slides
to change tune, its U-shaped tubes
forming an S or fetal coil of possibility

like a daughter pulling away, fists unclenching.

My late father played the trombone
for Scranton High's student orchestra, the one
football player who loved making music
more than blocking passes or sacking quarterbacks:
Curious boy running down the shape of
expectations trying to be more than tough.

The early trombone was called *sackbut,*
French for *saquer* (pull) and *bouter* (push), its one
repetitive movement to attach and detach.

Like siblings extend and slide
into each other's worlds until torsion
breaks the bonds, dislocates. Reality's funny

friction fails to hold papers in the mouth
of a clip. Productivity, portability, and loss are
the metal tongues of language—buzzing lips
of a mother who still feels small, her mouth
gripping the brass heart's bell rage between never
enough and hazy vibration of half-notes

like the paperclip I've now untwisted. Or acrobatic
Hebrew letters in a book on the table, the one
with words right to left for *your father*
and *fog*. Curious why they're spelled the same
but only one wears *nikudot* (vowels).
I ask my Israeli colleague:

How can a word have no vowels? How
can such different words be clipped
together?

This ancient language is an Abjad, one
whose vowels are discarded, unnecessary
because we Hebrew speakers just know
where the vowels would be. She laughs,
no one would mistake fog for father.

Most orchestras seat three trombones
like my parents' pit of two sons and me, the one
who's unclipped from our family, unfolded

and picking locks, reaching hard places. Fog horns
pull ships to shore while bugles push graveside
for those left off life's page, muted.

An only daughter is the truth-teller, down
like a family wound, wounded and unwound.

To be a simple paper clip found is to be
Le Trombone in red script or a vowel in an abjad
language, ancient and holy. How so much
power is found in small things.

In Response to *The Atlantic*'s "Elite College Students Who Can't Read Books," October 1, 2024

Rose Horowitch isn't wrong / my honors-level girls would even trip over her last name / but they'd recognize *wrong* / a sight word / backslashes too / like the bullet points they favor / but a poem lies among the detritus / another word they'd skim past / the debris of high school English / neither of which is 'useful to their careers' / like they are to mine / words yes / but I mean students / for whom I indeed "thinned out" the syllabus / twenty-six years teaching and today it's a quiz on Dillard's *Pilgrim at Tinker Creek* / 5. Discuss the significance of ants / "the little guys work so hard" / 'ants symbolize community' / wrong / "small but mighty"/ again wrong / my colleague leans on me for expecting they'd actually read it / like they are prey I have failed to catch / "what do insects matter to teenage girls" / Rose and Dillard and I know / ants don't have to catch their prey / "in the spring they swarm over newly hatched / featherless birds in the nest / and eat them bite by bite" / like a syllabus thinned / books unread / or a fact most useful to any woman's career

Sonnet Where Rhyme and Meter Fail the Poem Like Capitalism Fails the Child

Mom said just drink two glasses of water
to stop the hunger and quiet complaints.
He'd dream of shopping with bags of quarters.
She'd wake—cold sounds of copper down the drain.

Whispers: *get whatever you want I'll pay*
fill his brain, make-believe making him sane.
Home-sweet-home of red velvet cake doorway,
up taffy stairs with rails of candy cane

while Twinkie-brick walls lead to sweet cream
rooms. She feeds emptiness with chocolate chips
and tries to maintain it—poverty's dream,
but she falls awake. Childhood *drip-drips*

like change from his pocket. Dreams grow shorter:
What we need is to drink some more water.

To My Step Father-in-Law

who said there was demon energy in my house that he'd read about it in *World Magazine* who said reading *Harry Potter* to my daughter opened the door for Satan which is why bad things were happening / like the wind-slam window shredding my finger to the bone like my son's hamster biting bacteria into my blood like my torn meniscus from standing after folding laundry like my spontaneous coronary artery dissection / to that step father-in-law who taught his PhD wife to be more agreeable and speak when spoken to and always respond *Sure!* with a smile to whatever cockamamie idea he proposed / to the step father-in-law who claimed my anxiety and depression were not symptoms of an overwhelmed and under-supported mother of three teaching all day and tutoring all night to make ends meet but rather the symptoms of an ungrateful heart / to this step father-in-law whose solution to demon energy was submission to the headship of my husband / to you step-father-in-law for your idea of a portable mini-dishwasher to shut me up / oh step-father-in-law who promised we would be set for life when you were gone—did you really leave us only a shoebox of Iraqi Dinars obsolete and valued at .00076 of the U.S. Dollar / and to my mother-in-law who went before him—did you smile and say *Sure!* when he wrote that into your wills?

What She Learns

at 2.
She had legs designed for go-go dancing.

at 4.
She should let him into the bathroom with her to make sure she washed.

at 5.
She must be demon-possessed.

at 7.
She shouldn't hide in the neighbor's tree house all day.

at 8.
She better never write the *F* word on the blackboard at school again.

at 10.
Friends move away.

at 12.
Her messy body bleeds: a bathroom scale reigns her in.

at 14.
She cannot hold her alcohol.

at 16.
That's what she gets for wearing a short skirt.

at 18.
No means nothing.

at 21.
She is a phony feminist and can't be trusted to choose her own lovers.

at 24.
To drop out.

at 28.
To exercise longer and harder than most people.

at 38., 44
She's a mother without a mother. She's a wife without a husband.

at 53.
She's a bitch for leaving everyone behind.

Sonnet XIV

Born to T___ and J___: one girl. Peabody,
Massachusetts, in a split-level. Two
Brothers, T___ and C___, stole her dolls at three.
Four, and W___ stole her tricycle too:

The scar settled into her cheek at five.
The year they moved to Hong Kong, she was six:
Yelled *there's no God*—seven, apologized.
Back in the States, eight, to celebrate—Twix

Bars! They yelled *fat*. Spin the bottle at nine
In Cincinnati, at ten she lost friends.
Eleven and useless, deep in her mind;
Not thin, twelve's body curtsied ballet's end.

Thirteen and Old Milwaukee Light she drank;
By fourteen every girl knows life point-blank.

Meditation on Parenting

Parenthood is a tropical evergreen
bearing Titian-tint fruit, pear-shaped
marañon forming drupes
that birth a single cashew seed. Like these

cashews beneath apples, our children
spend years with us. Anacardium,
they exist outside our hearts no matter bold
blooming efforts to snug them in.

Known in Portuguese as *acaju,*
or that which produces itself, cashews
grow double shells and potent skin
not unlike a daughter who stretches further

away behind her bedroom door.
Kidney-shaped fruit a sudden swimming pool
my boy's aureate body enters
like a song. His tantrums of urushiol

oil sweat poison-ivy like cashews
which must be roasted with protective gloves.
Unbearable toxins, parenting—careful
processing is crucial. Failing again,

I am monkey-rose apple, false fruit
and useless. How I've treated my own parents.
When it drops below 10°C,
cashew trees freeze, are replaced.

What Never Seems to Happen

The husband and kids drive off, they leave
me in total peace. This time
it is late July. If I think of
them now, I smell the chlorine,
chaos, and sunscreen. I'm happy
being here alone. Always the corner of
the couch. Slide open
every window, and I tuck feet under
my thigh until the breeze lulls
the dogs to sleep. The sky is
now indigo, the trees proud. Savoring
the sound of my neighbor's wind
chimes, I begin to write
what I hope is a poem so honest it
leaves my heart empty.

To Be a Word in a Poem

rather than a human on this earth—
to be a well-chosen word,
useful and aware of exactly what I am, my purpose. To be
united with other words by some mad maternal creator
who wraps us in tenderness or watches
from the kitchen window as we rhythm up the treehouse ladder,
or leap into nylon lines of hammock stanzas
when it's time to pause.

To be a word in an Ilya Kaminsky poem
rather than a citizen of late-stage capitalism—
content watching language dive and breach,
my sole desire to know every sign
for *peace*, *home*, and *dance*. Together we could be
a phrase *(forgive us)*. Some twilight nights, I'd walk down
the page to borrow cups of rhyme, a stick of meter. We'd
wave to each other from the edge of our page.
At block parties, we'd dance multisyllabic, staccato, Skeltonic.

To be a word in a Chen Chen poem
rather than a body in this world—
neither isolated nor oppressed nor a vessel of self-hate.
Non-binary, asexual, aromantic,
queerplatonic, and celebrating ambiguities. Complex.
We'd print and press between connotation and denotation,
where etymology matters. Sharing
letters and sounds, we would allow no bans, protect all trans.
Perhaps we could be *the hot pink*. Resist
and refuse objectification to embrace the fluidity

of being a word in an Eavan Boland poem
rather than a citizen of Oligarchy—
where greed grabs the land, where violence claws
at the weak while elites ascend,
feeding off the sweat of us. Here, where
the promises of liberty break apart,
and meaning like justice fades, muffled by the shrill
gleam of power. We'd whisper,
what else could we have done? Where speech
is drowned by the tide
of tyrants as inequality pollutes.

Oh, to be one word in the first draft of a poem
rather than an entry in a dictionary—
more than something monitored and approved
by OED's corpus analysis. To be
fluid, shaped by context, rhythm, to be
whispered, shouted, or contracted. To be a place
holder but not know it. Where
there's no such thing as a better word, only truer.

How I'd rather be a word in a poem
than the poet—to be said out loud,
underlined, and highlighted. Shared and spoken
until tucked between cool white sheets, to meet the sleep
of the unread. To wake
and walk where Carolyn Forché's drums
are buried. To live
a thousand lives where tensions and translations

mean existence. I'd live a thousand lives
as a word in verse.
I'd climb bookmark mast-heads
to watch and wait
for the next school of letters breaching, rising
against the censors, the squall of hard-forged lies. When
the world drowns, I'd be
a small part of something beautiful finally,
forever turning flukes. To have
bones set by grief, vowels cradled by consonants,
plosives ready to burst, and fricatives slipping
into surprise. To be wise as Wittgenstein's *meaning is use*—

Cold-blooded

I turn off my phone after another berating from my mother / Go back to reading *The Best of It,* unraveled again this November / My son's fire-bellied toads bask in the blur of artificial heat, need live crickets / This place reeks of mythical morass, both clean & fetid / I locate a sharp knife, pop the inflated bladder from Alan's Pet Shop while Shostakovich pours from the neighbor's window / Commotion, the toads upend their porcelain pond, use heart-shaped pupils to hunt prey / Kay Ryan & I burrow under blankets of tension, dissent, & defiance / We enter her poem, that line where the turtle is thankful to live below *luck-level* / A strange virtuoso, I too am *graceless,* climbing toward *sweet grass* I'll someday find / Like a piccolo's high C, the larger toad inhales a cricket, pleased with his own yellow-black speed / I could live alone & like it.

Re-Reading *Beowulf,* I Remember My Mother's Address Book

I

atop her stack of cascading bills and letters
like a Polly Pal paperweight or pink
and white gingham kenning its mylar cover

uncharacteristic of the middle-aged woman
gate-keeping my firedrake adolescence
this blond breaker of rings with curved bang

bowl-cut hair helmet as gleamy and round
as her ivory bracelet battle tusks from Thailand
an elephant graveyard stacked like slain

warriors pitching about the Valhalla of her
nacreous forearm and wrist this poached score
of my childhood was a cacophonous death rattle

II

Mornings brought finger snaps *be quiet can't you
see I'm on the phone* and every brandish of her fist
heads will roll and the ease of her ball point

strike-through heavy and scriptorium-slow across
the pages moments after hearing the news
of the latest friend or relative no longer around

fingering A-Z tabs for names and addresses
like my godparents Peter and Mary Kunda
at 543 Prospect Avenue Scranton PA now gone

III

Into the earth and out of her cache of Ks they lay
near cousin ~~Frances Klein~~ and ~~Dr. Koursh~~
each donning my mother's skull and cross-outs

her casual delineation between the living
and the dead between Christmas cards and ancient
history swift as the tornado in '79 descending

moments after I stepped from the afternoon
bus with Jill Connors when her own chimney's
brick struck her head—I wanted to empty her

backpack and take her new supply of erasable
pens pooling like Freyja's tears the only
hope I had against my mother's hand in the Cs

Hunger

I keep Darkness well fed.
It needs me.
Sometimes breakfast:
        Smoked grief
        two minutes in the pot.
        Hash browns
        like childhood, shredded.
        Goji berry smoothies,
        magenta rivers from
        father's buckle.

When adventurous, I
take Darkness to the Farmer's Market:
        Locally grown intentions
        simmering in butter
        and fresh rage
        before quenelles of bitter cream.
        Oyster mushrooms
        braised in misplaced loyalties.

Most days,
I work with whatever's in the cupboards:
        The last two gripes,
            a canister of seasoned panic crumbles.
            A sleeve of unhinged macaroons.
            Cayenne to match
            a lover's infidelities. I ignite

Darkness in me;
keep my keeper feasting. Fasting,
I make a New Year's resolution:
            Subscribe to *Southern Living;*
            binge Food Network
            because the way to survive
            a bottomless world
            is to keep from being
            swallowed.

Meditation on Selective Memory Begins with Jimmy Carter

who can identify every bird
      in the trees of Plains GA.

Sweet songs of indigo buntings to
      yellow-throated warblers

ruby-throated hummingbirds &
      purple martins. Sometimes

vermilion flycatchers appear in
      fall & winter. I on the other

hand can identify every episode
      of *Murder, She Wrote:*

like "Birds of a Feather" or "Murder
      Takes the Bus" & "The Corpse

Flew First Class" then "Snow White,
      Blood Red," my soft spot

watching fictional murders solved
      by a stately woman wearing

well-plumed suits. My knowledge
      of Cabot Cove ME

rivals Jimmy Carter's knowledge of birds—

& I wonder what it says about us,
    the things we remember.

What it says about choosing to love
    something so deeply

it nests forever in the mind. Yet who
    will recall the name of

a shelter dog who is head-shy &
    anxious around men,

or a dog found on the highway who
    is still good with kids? What
does it mean to discard something
    meant only to be loved,

like the mayor of a MS town did:
    ordering thirteen dogs

in the Montgomery County pound
    useless, to be taken out

& shot? Dead, unlike GA birds
    alive in Jimmy Carter's mind.

SELF Portrait as Character List

MOTHER—one diet pill at lunch will do the trick / always wear lipstick—Quiet.

BROTHER—a walk the day before I started high school / be like Kathy M and not like Leanne T / girls are just categories—Leave me alone.

SELF—compulsively exercises / projects / perfects the inner critic / read *Always Know What to Say: Easy Ways to Approach and Talk to Anyone* / because something.

Chicago PSYCHIATRIST—questions exploring bisexuality are funny maybe you're a tri-sexual 'cuz you'll try anything—Quiet.

Santa Monica barre INSTRUCTOR—corrects my C curls and single pulses then squeals I love a project / pushes on my feet while I lie in savasana / gonna transform your body if it's the last thing I do—Leave me alone.

1st HUSBAND—budget with Quicken / you should read Dave Ramsey and save receipts—Quiet.

Christian HEAD of SCHOOL—welcomes me to the faculty with a hardback of *The Excellent Wife: A Biblical Perspective* / because something about me.

BARTENDER at Cork & Flame—lick the salt then suck the lime / comps a slice of toffee layer cake in exchange for a smile—Leave me alone.

That EDITOR—never accepts my work / almost but it feels like there's a moral instead of letting the reader appreciate the messy characters / something says—Quiet.

My CHILDREN, also my STUDENTS—rewrite the script.

American Tragedy

The CHORUS of women
toss from their throats
a wish to reverse the rivers
unwind all Corinths
like Medea's smoky braids

When I left Chicago
to braid a life in Los Angeles
after the '94 earthquake
the La Cienega off-ramp
crumbled into concrete oracle

or ode: freeways are feathers
home is potion & myth
Faith is a steel blade we choose
& rivers don't flow uphill
—but the ground can shift

The CHORUS of Proud Boys
on a cold 6th of January
became a swarm of chants
riot gear & rifles smoky
torrent of rage unbraided

Golden Trowel; Cross Country Move, L.A. to Georgia

after Sharon Olds

An eight-hour drive becomes twelve with no   stop;
your son sobs in the Kia's third row, whispers   *don't do it.*
Cat on his lap, head against glass, and   you are going
east almost to the South Carolina border   to do things
to people and animals   you cannot imagine you would ever do.

BEGINNINGS

Drove my car to leave this disaster.
I've mistaken your love as laughter,
And California's colder than last year.
Far from you so maybe I'll stay here.

—Michael Marcagi, "American Romance"

Parable with Flags, Humidity & Loss

In our Kia, the final odyssey Atlanta to Augusta,
    I made note of the distance. Delusion burst,
Atlanta was not a viable airport option. LAX had been
    a neighbor, mere blocks down Manchester.
A braided nymph appeared on the side of I-20, asked
    what the fuck are you doing? Disappeared
into her cave. We crossed into Georgia where the flags
    were flying. Trump, stars and bars, *Don't Tread*
on Me, Go Dawgs, and Blue Lives Matter. So Proud
    Boy bumper stickers really did exist unlike
Yak racks or the Mississippi River water line. Gun racks
    on trucks rising in tidal Dixie ferocity today.
Pulling into our new driveway, the car was silent
    as a sacrifice or regret. Each kid opened
a door to the Southern summer's maw. Cruel-greeting
    blade. I offered an invocation to the Muse,
sing in me something familiar. L.A. kids don't understand
    humidity, damp and unnerving. They unfolded
into the assault of reality's new address. To make it
    here meant giving something up, memory maybe.
Like any good mother weaving optimism for months,
    I taught them how to unweave, buy time.

Candice

I too dislike it.
Embarrassed by the effort
a mouth exerts
to say my name,
to pronounce what amounts to me—

seven little signifiers
clawing the throat
like seven days of destruction.

A mother is a world
that gives as well as takes.

My other name—*Rotten rotten rotten.*

Waning into a sliver of self
I disappear beneath the phonetic expanse
fricative & voiceless. Float
the hard & soft of it.

Who can reach across the seas of mother & daughter?

Climb my silent *e*.
Birth something from the softer *c*.
Find the agency of *i*—like a stiff middle
finger to her *d-n-a* & land
like a cat on its feet
curling feral not fetal into hard *C*.

I am plosive. Click a half-moon trick
& unwrap this cocoon.

Remember a name is not a person
& *Mother* is just a name.

Tonight, My Friend Shows Me How to Give Myself a Hug

When I tell her sometimes I
push myself too hard in a
workout, elevate my heart rate
because I want to induce
cardiac arrest and be found
slumped over the handlebars
of my Peloton, she suggests
I need to self-soothe
in those dark moments and
she pushes back from her screen
to show me one strategy
she likes—*first you stretch
your right arm palm facing
out, then your left and clasp
together.* For a moment
there we stand, two middle-
aged women on a Zoom happy
hour doing some woo woo
Hokey Pokey, trying to turn
my life around when she says

*Now scoop your hands into
your body, up to your chest
and squeeze yourself tight.*
We smile at each other and
hug ourselves a surprisingly
long time: her, pleased to give
the gift of touch, and me
imagining myself forever in
this position, six feet under.

The Art of Encouragement

—I would have cheered her on from the front row,
my mother's hair in a clutch
of blond wisps waiting before the bee's judges,

the auditorium of Stonington Middle School.

Her eyes sharp as talons focused, masking the fear
of classmates' laughter, of six sisters' Scylla-carnival
criticism when the gritty disembodied voice crackled
electric through dust and adolescence:

Antarctica. Your word is Antarctica, Jeannie.
Disappointment is a long walk home. She forgot the *c,*

somewhat silent gull of a letter, third in the alphabet
and shape of Pawcatuck farmhouse sleep with Beverly and Dawny,
curled in a shared twin. *C* like a cracked egg or initial

that decades later would crown the name she gave me: *Candice,*
third child. Only daughter, another difficult word.
Is motherhood just mile after mile of getting it wrong?

I think of the marathoners today in Los Angeles,
crowds cheering along Hollywood Boulevard. The wheelchair
and hand crank participants, the ones with carbon
fiber C-curves. Even those suckered into running,

first-timers wide-eyed as a girl in a spelling bee.

To encourage someone, according to poet Maggie Nelson,
is the *unceasing rigorous work of a lifetime.*

I think tonight of the Big Bear bald eagles, Jackie and Shadow,
whose three eggs will not be hatching after all
the thunder-snow and thirty-thousand YouTube followers
whose hearts break with mine.

Please Lord, let just one pip break out with a newly formed egg
    tooth,

perfect tool atop its tiny bill to puncture the membrane
and take a first breath like the lifetime
of encouragement some daughters wear. I too have
feathers I'll never preen. My mother is eighty,
with the egg tooth of an addled eaglet.

Her sister-brood's eyes still gritty shells of judgment.
The embarrassment I am for flying far from the Wilkinson
ways, their headless tree unraveling nests

built from *you bitch, you owe me,* and *you'll regret this.*
I soar thermal updrafts, incubate
a disembodiment from that shallow Antarctic ice.

In the coming days, Jackie and Shadow
will over-incubate. Do they hear us holding out for a miracle?
Even so they will make a slow withdrawal, leaving.

A Gift

after James Wright

Just down Route 15 to Fork Union, Virginia,
Between Weber City and Dixie, we settle
Into a farmhouse Airbnb. Run past the pool
And fire pit as dusk prances gently,
Inviting us into the meadow. And the manes
Of two Chincoteague ponies ripple
With joy. They have come gaily out of the stable
To welcome my son and daughter.
Who's more enchanted? Two jaded city kids
Climb the barbed fence into a pasture
Where horses have grown bored of grazing
On tall fescue and red top. Ears forward
And neighing, they cannot hide their excitement
For visitors. Like two dew-laden lilies,
They bow with the heaviness of need. The evening
Mist answers afternoon's rain, rises like tears
In a mother's eyes. The chestnut one
Nuzzles my girl, twelve and awkward as a foal.

The bay's eyes meet my son's and brighten
With recognition, each mane more wild
Than the other's. One as certain of its future
As the other is uncertain. I would like
To hold the slenderness of this moment, brush
The lustrous tail of adolescent hope. Ride
This assurance that loneliness is not permanent.
That beauty comes in its own time. And how
With the break of a gallop, three years pass:
My son is a young man now working
The grill at Sno-Cap Drive-In. Leaning into its
Counter is a young waitress. Beauty arrives
Like dusk. DMs him, *hey you seem really cool.*

Cool

I used to think my oldest brother
was the epitome of it
in his hush puppies and tweed,
taking D___ to Homecoming,
real life prince and princess.
Until he left for college,
and I took his room, the waterbed,
removed Farrah Fawcett, Adrienne
Barbeau, and Cheryl Tiegs
from his walls. After tossing
sports bra and fuchsia leggings
onto his electric guitar and amp,
I took my rightful seat as man
of our suburban house atop
the stairs, left of the laundry chute.
At his desk with a map of the world
under its glass, for once I was
cool. Staring at the USSR. I knew
ICBMs were pointed at America,
ready. How could I feel safe
up against something so huge?

Opening my brother's sock drawer,
I found a deck of playing cards:
52 Vintage Nudes and Pin-Ups
between tube socks and argyles.
Could he be *un*cool? Lately,
we rarely text each other,
only updates about our kids.
He keeps it brief and impersonal,
detached like he's locked inside
childhood's room with posters,
playing cards, and Led Zeppelin.
Forever two doors down from him, I
wonder what occurs. Today,
I text my chapbook is out,
and he plays that one deft card
from an old standby pack—*Cool.*

Flesh and Bone

They think it's been months since my mom tried to contact me.
Cousins say she's reaching out to connect. I say it's been years
of *you are such a bitch* and *this whole family is done with you.*

My dead mother-in-law tells me I'm too resourceful to let it
suck my will to live; I hear more work. She says step back.
Says observe the process and sends me an email from above,

her preferred after-life method. The subject: Snow & Peace.
A picture of the oak in her ghost yard, an amuse-bouche
wearing a floor length gown of white pin-dotted snow accented

with one green birdhouse. Frosted cupcake feeder, it says
here, here is sustenance. Echoes how I want to take
all my dead mother-in-law offers through the marrow of my mind.

Mother's way of comforting was declaring me her own
flesh and blood. Nailing me to her. There is a bird called
    lammergeier, German for lamb vulture. It raptors the bones of
    carrion,

drops them onto flat rocks to expose the marrow.
My mother-in-law's ghost is one of these bone droppers. Asks
what I gain from allowing my mother's opinions to define me.

Am I a cloth napkin of a girl dropped beside bone China
where marrow has been sucked from the calf's flesh, just a baby,
cross-cut? *Osso buco,* Italian for bone with a hole.

The spongy cake of bones consists of hematopoietic cells
from *poesies,* ancient Greek for the emergence of something
that did not previously exist; also, poetry. That flesh and blood

is made of poetry, that lines break like bones, that I emerged
from the syntax of a mother who drops *rotten rotten
daughter.* Will I never find sustenance? I find

my mother's wedding announcement, 1964, *Scranton Times:*
Cake topper of a woman, she wore a Chantilly lace
and white silk organza chapel gown with a scalloped neck.

Her headpiece of sheer rosettes with a large flower on top
was edged in seed pearls. What about that seedless bird feeder
nailed to a frozen oak somewhere on heaven's peninsula?
Peninsula, Latin for almost an island; or a daughter.

I worry about the birds. Remember they prepare for the cold,
stockpile seeds, and pack pockets of air around their bodies.

Because Your Husband's Shirt is Ironed

is the punchline
of his assistant basketball coach
meeting me finally
that's how I knew you were in town

I politely smile
turn to hug my former student
who's often ostracized for being queer
the lunch crew

misses you, sixteen-year-old Jaden tells me
I hug him again
quickly before the tip-off
to confirm my appreciation for the wrinkles

he causes in the Immanuel Presbyterian
private school fabric

later at the Pizza Joint in downtown
Augusta my son orders
a large pie and extra garlic knots

rather than the garden salad my daughter chooses

dry no dressing
a week before the Homecoming dance
and eight moms start
a text thread to make plans

one of them texts *I'm sorry*
promises to be more organized next year

I retort *let's remember the dads*
don't have a Homecoming
dance group chat—receive no response

O how the South hates a wrinkle

On Democracy

                Its chartreuse needles
bundle in waxy triplicate, this loblolly
in front of me. Pine sharp
are today's Tennessee three—
Pearson, Jones, & Johnson.

The sun now greets
a familiar Southern covenant
atop our morning back deck.
We splinter red cedar & sleepy
as Nashville dreams a country music scene:
two Black Representatives
expelled for protesting.

Nashville's hills tumble like innocents
murdered under a garden sky,
& the Cumberland
rises before merging with the Ohio.

                A Kel-Tec SUB-2000,
the shooter was a tornado moving
Ionic limestone columns,
razing 3rd graders & their teacher,
a beloved custodian & head of school.

Dionysus' words stopped Tyrrhenian pirates
to save Democracy once.
Can cones bring hope in a backyard tree,
are seeds flowering
over bark's ochre scales? Or
is it all just filthy pine tar,
the legacy of early European colonists?

A bald eagle seventy feet up, incubates
three eggs in a loblolly where

my eyes land. In Tennessee, on America,
& all the guns.
River by river, tree by tree,
lawmaker by lawmaker—
                      a few of us not sold out.

I See Fallen Trees

like wings along Mullikin Road
north of downtown Augusta
where the I-520 haloes Georgia
and South Carolina hard
hit by Helene these loblolly pines
dismembered by chainsaws
piled beside downed power lines

when I remember my best
friend's kitchen table mid-80s
42" beveled pine wood circle
where we gathered like a coven
calling Ticketmaster on rotary
for Madonna's *Like a Virgin* tour
and the scent of sourdough
encouraged our faith in flying
toward whatever we wanted

a simple slice of warm bread
on a lazy Susan in Ohio
from my friend's mother selfless
as a cloud until her husband
entered the scene licking his fingers
stiff trunk of three phalanges
which he plunged into the loaf
corner to corner and across
tornadoing holes of destruction

like the lawns of my neighbors
where trees used to stand
because that was his message
to his wife who should fall in line
and not eat the bread to keep
to her diet and lose that weight
which he reminded her of
by stacking 5 lb. bumper plates
onto the table like the logs

cut and stacked along Mullikin
thin remainders of once towering
loblollies like young girls' wings
by a hard reality newly crushed

Into the Womb of Air

The wind is the better lover and the better mother. I said the wind is the one who softens into a breeze when it's tenderness you need the wind is the better lover and the better mother when it caresses the back of your neck and whispers affirmations like you've never heard before the wind will let you know it's present without fanfare or love-bombing or fear or obligation and guilt the opposite of a covert narcissist lover or borderline personality mother the wind can sway the lines into an ovation in bark-needle praise of private victories and occasionally pick up its step to rattle this world from sleep like a fucking good lover like your fantasy mother to remind you that your living body your very body you've been taught to hate the thighs and belly and arms your mother marked with pen *measure twice cut once* so you could imagine taking up less space slicing away the heavy flesh that body must be celebrated before it's swept away into the molecules that body must expand and rise as byproduct of the sun a child of uneven topography wind is the planet's lover eternal my mother ideal so I turn my face into it.

Mothers & Daughters

arrange themselves
like butterflies near petals
of fleur-de-lis curtains
delicate as I'd like to be
scalloped porcelain
bowl beside a tiny spoon
on the buffet
this March morning
at the Monteagle Inn

I'd much rather be
that mother in the corner
whose daughter leans in
or the one whose daughter
scoops berries
perfect globed jewels
red-blue-black ready
for breakfast's snowfall
of granola clouds of yogurt

rather than me
alone at this stupid table
Mother's Weekend
waiting for my daughter
who may oversleep

and miss this tenderness
of conversation
the tinkling of forks
like fairy chimes heralding
chiffon delights of
motherhood I could

be delicate but am brutal
like my mother
a still life in crinoline
cold sip of coffee am I
the song of a window
wasp for texting
where the hell are u
though unlike my mother
I never hit send

Photosynthesis Reversed

    You were chlorophyll   *thick coiled garden shells*
       Mother, our ways   *slice themselves thin*
    revealing true colors   *honey-curled days now*
    terrible wild carmine   *shorter and shorter*
      I take the encore   *and deep flowering*
  forth into sweet autumn   *until I close off*
       these veins, shed   *one plush bed, humus*
    dark, organic matter   *I am daughter and mother*
a decaying pile of twigs   *who dreams of protecting*
   my differentiated self   *never again found*
    succumbing to your   *overbearing sugar waltz*

Playing Hide 'n Seek with My Father's Ghost

the blue-sky gleams [_____]
from behind the oak tree [_____]
like it's fed by the stream [_____]

     on the day my father dies
      we believed they'd never find us
       our hide 'n seek dream

the green leaves hang [_____]
giving shade to the brush below [_____]
rocks disrupt the rugged waves [_____]

     like memories or pain
      shhhh
       ready or not here they come

the waterfall crashes [_____]
the bottom where it collects [_____]

     he holds my hand
      squeezes i love you

into a tranquil place [_____]
where nature is free [_____]
stripped bare [_____]
with unending flow [_____]

      we are found
      i flee to safety but he is caught
   all of us run
      one game away from being It

Family Fun and Sparklers for the Kiddos

Fourth of July. The husband-and-wife sheriffs next door, Blue Lives Matter eclipsing their American flag by inches and implied fuck-yous, always bring their A game. It was 99 degrees around 9pm on our modest Savannah River adjacent cul-de-sac overrun with lawn cars and boats. Chapman, the husband, lost his leg from a drunk driver collision and 22 subsequent failed surgeries to save it. He was moving slowly with the prosthetic C-curve, his French Fork beard, and a 12-pack of Rolling Rock. Mallory, the wife, had squeezed every fleshy blessing from the Good Lord into her American flag bikini. She served as the barefoot pyrotechnics' dominatrix, calling shots and correcting placements. Fluent in F-Bomb, many an unsuspecting neighborhood kid—mouth open and eye on their own parent—has frozen under her tutelage. When Chapman took issue with Mallory's mortar-and-shell decisions, snuffing out several small fires on our neighbors' yard notwithstanding, he let the unkind Georgia night know she was 'too fucking drunk' to carry out her responsibilities with a lighter. She pitched her Bic torch like a skipping rock down the pavement, threatening one small child's ankles save for a parkour leap. She ended the discussion with a winning flare: 'Shut the fuck up, you one-legged Jackass!' After the show, their 12-year-old daughter worked the push broom from asphalt to curb like a clean street was her heart's desire.

Chronic Prepositions

Small / many & often are these funny words we're tasked to memorize / rhymes like hickory-dickory dock / the mouse ran [up down to through beside from] the clock / relationship words & a child's song about a terrified mouse / like a fish out of water / today I am shit out of luck / for inheriting my mother's degenerative arthritis / keeping me under the weather rather than over the moon / with pain not without / each swollen juncture between bones / ball & joint hickory-dickory / a mouse climbing through me / his tiny knapsack full / of time location & motion / maneuvering with ease unlike me / weakening / unable to turn the knob / I use both hands to step from the house / over the threshold / past the pain of a body on fire / a body like a door I cannot open / a door with a window through which I see my mother's ghost free of pain / climbing out of life's clock / I ache alongside this funny rhyme / & want to run [up down to through beside from] her voice / the rodent under my skin / between the bones find one small object: daughter / of the preposition: mother / throbbing *with, without—*

Renewable Energy

Pedaling the Sold-Out Show
ride with @PelotonJenn
this Sunday morning
forty-five minutes with
Bruce at the Meadowlands
weeks before the '09 demo
and the crowd detonates
during his performance

I keep a steady 1-2-1-2
noticing my performance
is thirty watts lower than
six months earlier when
my own stadium crumbled
from the death of my father
something about his body
lowered there to the drums
of twenty-one guns and

here Clemons' sax helps
teach me the higher output
then had nothing to do with
endurance and everything
to do with the fire of loss—

grief is always the culprit
keeping its steady cadence

while the world's engineers
explore renewable energy
in rough taut baritone notes
in jeans and a short-sleeve
black shirt half buttoned
with a nineteen-piece band
inside Elm Grove Cemetery
the sold-out show of me

don't you see grief here—
the only sustainable resource

Full Self-Driving

April's rhythmic ticks whining along
Columbia County's fall line stitch duets

with beautyberry and golden ragwort
while Bermuda grass hushes the suburbs.

This morning, I hear the cicadas' engine;
I stare out to the great flora unknown,

which tells me there was an emerging.
But these are not June's dog day locusts.

Each brood, what? Roman numerals, ok.
This May will be our twenty-third year

in marriage's hardwood forest. We end
our own cycle making no more slits

in tree branches. Divorce is the egg nest
now. This morning the U.S. government's

auto safety agency probes whether Tesla
did enough to ensure drivers were paying

attention. No Full Self-Driving taxis yet, Musk
reports. Autopilot recalls, something about

how it senses human torque on the wheel
and a dead motorcyclist, only twenty-eight.

The affidavit revealed a fifty-three-year-old
driver trusted the machine to drive for him.

Trust: is there anything more dangerous?
Full Self-Driving: a total reliance on sensory

input to plot a path and control direction,
or permission to disengage—at which point

lovers no longer see nor hear each other. July
and cicadas quiet, bodies drop by the road.

[C]ars Poetica

Imagine
a world where automobiles
are not named
after endangered animals,
virtues, & forces
of nature.

The Tahoe
is no mirror-glass lake
of green. The Avalanche
doesn't tremble
or threaten mortal drifts.
Honestly, the Leaf?
Why can't I fall

into
an anthologized sunset-
orange Sonnet,
drive off the lot
waving farewell
to the balladeer salesman,
singing in *abab* Blue
Book meter?

Perhaps
lease a Pantoum
& always make perfect
time. Or finance
the metallic gold Sestina—
six-wheel drive
& sleek envoi
with *such great lines!*

Truth is
I'd rather bike
a Haiku's
syllabic gear-switch
5th to 7th to 5th.
Wheels like seasons
turning through
kigo, cherry blossoms
& snow. I'd coast
kireji, hands off the bars—
cutting the moon.

Not for the Faint of Heart

Rushing to the cardiologist down Fury's Ferry in an Uber
With Eldon listening to Dexys Midnight Runners
Belt out *Come on Eileen* as he slows and half-turns to me
The universal pose for I'm about to ask you a question
To in fact ask me if I know what the lyrics are all about

And I admit ignorance while tapping my feet to the jaunty
Beat of this shiny well-loved oldie but goodie that opens
The door to the early 80s me in Jennie Olson's basement
Where we spun faster and faster to the urgent horns
Weeks before she moved to Pennsylvania and her brother

Pins me to the Sycamore around back by the empty shed
Midnight after packing the house his tongue spins down
My throat his summer fist feeling up my terry-cloth polo
The one from Lake of the Ozarks Tan-Tar-A Resort shop
To find my private twelve-year-old chest rhythming fear

That night I swore my heart stopped from a swirl of desire
Mixed with disgust and Eldon steers me to his question
Where I'm fifty-three and off to get a boring echocardiogram
Ma'am it's about the desire to remove her red dress
I chuckle and agree politely that it's creepy and no one cares

To question familiar things like a best friend's older brother
Or the heart's structure because chambers vessels and valves
Clenched into a fist-sized red dress exist to tap and run
Us into existence every morning until something unexpected
From around back tears the artery and splits a problematic flap

I find myself with a stent and follow up with some Dr. Miller
Who unlike Eldon does not show up so it's Stacy who does
My echo today—*Undress from the waist up*—half-turned I
Ask how she can read the screen know where to click and drag
For measurements also what are those blue and red splatters

Pollacking about my chest in an iambic jaunt she chuckles
She's studied the heart for thirty-six years she's majored
In cardiac imaging that the blue and red are blood cells
From the Doppler just like we see on the Weather Channel
I go quiet thinking of the tiny storms patterned inside me

And ask what she likes about the heart to which she obliges
It's so small and yet so complex this ever-shifting always
Twisting sexy little pop song of life like adolescence in a way
I offer Stacy who ignores me tapping more keys and staring
At my embarrassing blob of life askew and displayed in gray

A Tale of Two Cities; or, Alerts from Citizen App While I Commute

Los Angeles, CA.

"Report of suspicious box spilling pink sand" on 3rd and Broadway; Citizen commenter suggests this is fairy dust.

"Man carrying feces, barking at woman" in Silicon Beach.

"Woman wielding a machete at Wendy's, wants free Frosty."

"Man hit woman with bag of coins, shouting Fight On" at MacArthur Park Metro station.

"Firefighters responding to reports of a man hog tied in a closet."

Augusta, GA.

"Report of man assaulted with Bible" at Warren Baptist Church.

"Lone chicken spotted on Fury's Ferry Road;" Citizen commenter responds, "that's my cock."

"Pick-up truck with teenagers wielding swords and Confederate flag" at Washington Road Wife Saver.

"Woman dragging deer carcass, wearing only XTRATUFs" down Mullikin Rd.

"Animal control responding to reports of wild pigs loose on Augusta National golf course."

To the Bros in My Row

after the news broke that Derek Chauvin had been stabbed in prison

since I sit in 13D
from Augusta to Charlotte

let me abide you
clean-shaven and taut
across 13A to F

since a thirty-minute flight counts for something

then let us breathe SkyMiles
flip pages in memoirs
reposition gently—

since we are fellow AAdvantage members

let me look away
from your NRA pin
and *American Rifleman,*
its eagle perched
on two rifles and a shield

accept the reality
we share this
tight space and quiet air

until you speak—

*stupid cultural
competency initiatives*

then *poor Derek*

—since thirty minutes count for something

I cannot abide you
clean-shaven and taut
across 13A to F

since you do have sensitivity
for Derek Chauvin
let the nose of this American
Eagle be

like a swift prison shank—
stabbing cirrus,
cumulonimbus

cutting these minutes until
we land

—the logic of some Southern men is what, again?

Yes, It Could

Monday at 10:15 am
Mindy, the Chief Operating Officer,
Ordered an Active Shooter
Drill. All teachers and students
Were reminded how to lockdown
The classrooms, the proper
Protocol of Run, Hide, Fight.
The loudspeaker sang,
*This is a drill, this is a drill, please
Lockdown, there is an active
Shooter on campus.* And one girl,
A sophomore in the third row
Of room 113 who has a C-,
Rolled her eyes, shouting for all
To hear: *Could this day get any worse?*

Back in Los Angeles

my Uber driver confesses
he walked out

of the *Barbie* movie incensed
at how boys were

portrayed claiming the scene
where a guy slaps

Barbie's ass is unrealistic
he tells me down the 405 Freeway

that never happens
so I ask him why I have a decade's

worth of therapy bills
and later I binge

videos of post-menopausal orcas
protecting their sons and

a *60 Minutes* segment
on the British zoologist Lucy Cooke

whose work with sloths
reminds me Darwin was a Victorian

man branding the female
species as a feminine

footnote to the masculine main event
oh how I want to see a man

call the female spotted hyena
passive coy and chaste

see her laugh in his face after biting it off

To Which a Celebration of Life

makes me cry on Zoom in L.A. while watching
The live NYC memorial for my dear friend
Sherry dead at 71 to which *Variety*'s obituary
Dubbed her merely the "Creator of *Kate & Allie*"

To which I couldn't help but laugh as her mother
Shared the time when Sherry was only four
And descended the stairs ready for pre-school
Wearing pastels and plaid and neon knee socks

To which her mother asked if she was sure
About wearing that motley combination in public
To which Sherry replied *The sooner you realize
I am not a reflection of you, the better.* To which

There's little mystery why thirty years ago
Rebellious alone and estranged from my own
Mother I found myself wanting to be with Sherry
In her presence at her house with her children

Both signifier and signified and now her oldest
Daughter gives the eulogy to which I remember
That one Halloween when Sherry transformed me
Into a flamboyant lion with punk rock wig-mane

Which I wore one night in my grad school class
Proud as fuck though my peers were freaked out
Discussing Lacan and Derrida with this big cat
To which Sherry later replied *That'll teach 'em.*

Epiphany After Missing Your Connecting Flight to Augusta Airport

In line at the ticket counter with a new blister after running in Birkenstocks from Gate B / *I can get you to Augusta tomorrow* / numb & lifeless like dead skin / you choose to fly back to L.A. rather than go / spiraling into shame & guilt / midnight slumped at Gate E8 / *you can't* / unlike everyone else in the terminal / *who can* / be lines of human verse a traveling momentum / while your overwhelm blocks / & grounds you / a text to your children expecting you / explaining anxiety / your daughter replies *I love you it's going to be ok* / & right then she is Charles Simic / so you soften the voice of self-judgment / board the hybrid vessel that is prose poetry / write a new layer

                        because arriving is always secondary

You listen to Pearl Jam (Live at Wrigley Field, 2016) as you fly back to L.A. tonight / not passing over the space your mind rents in the canals / where egrets told you *writing with narrative distance won't help* re-process the traumas / pretend they sing: *riding with Mary this chance ghost-kelp you bench press* / skip tracks to "Crazy Mary" / meditate on ghost-kelp / don't see roofs of strip malls, life in B minor beneath this flight / dream of McCready's fingers / consider writing a poem in first person POV / no unpleasant aerial view of your second home / ask *who isn't Crazy Mary* over the curve, drinking down the fields / body a tar paper soul-shack / when you land where you began

                               & Eddie Vedder meets you halfway

At a Local Wine Tasting, I Consider Divorce

That is, this Culver City sommelier serves a 2020 François Rousset-Martin 'Couvée du Professeur Sous-Roche' Savignin Cotes du Jura while explaining the alcohol that evaporates during the aging process is called the 'Angel's Share.'

Legend has it guardian angels sample and bless the wine, then take their portion to the heavens. The dynamic freshness of the ouillé releases hints of caramelization, doing the marl soils of the storied Château-Chalon appellation proud this Friday evening east of the 405.

I enjoy its long finish, learning "this wine could make a compelling marriage with the notoriously difficult-to-pair artichoke." Our host slides my French Wine Scholar friend and me tiny wings of Comté cheese to lift the complexity. I too have been difficult to pair,

have been in symbiosis with a wine cellar environment, breathing the ambient yeast of motherhood, changing physically and evaporating from a once-compelling marriage. Sample a year of separation in the City of Angels.

After twenty-six years in his Burgundian barrel under a vaulted ceiling, I am not a viticultural wonder nor a profoundly human expression but an absence. Mere product loss. In Whiskey distillation, the remaining drink is called the 'Devil's Cut.'

Dear Potential Lover, Don't Bother

unless your name is

    I am listening,
    I see you,
Or
    What do you need right now?

And even then, only if your middle name is

    Hold my hand under the gibbous moon.

Ecstatic Ghosts

My belly is the Savannah River

I mean to say my belly is soft & rippling
but the river captures it
       makes my point prettier

Stretch marks

I mean to say the map's perforated line
in the river divides me
       like Georgia from South Carolina

Did you know I was alive before I gave birth

       I was alive with abdominal muscles intact
       but then my belly filled with song

Ruins

I mean to say my belly was a venue
for Ella Fitzgerald & Cab Calloway & Louis Armstrong
       back in the day

Today

I mean to say my hips hold a shallow pond
abutting the scraggly woods

Have you visited Palmetto Park & Pond
on Carolina Springs Road

I know I hold no interesting history
            but something there is about a woman
            transcendent & emptied

of Ghosts

I mean to say a small patch of lawn in North Augusta
once held a thousand capacity dance hall

        but WWII birthed its need for men & the land
        was sold to a trailer park

A Mother Commutes from Georgia to L.A. for a Higher Paying Job

is the vanity plate she screws onto her imaginary self-driving '84 station wagon. The same way she applies black ebony Telescopic Lift to her lashes each morning, twisting expectations into five-pound bags of Bit-O-Honey. Like the one she carried into the Appalachian Trail as a child, losing a tooth in corn syrup taffy under the forest cover of a sugar maple.

Play stupid games, win stupid prizes, her father had told her. That piece of her youth, orphan chiclet tooth, entombed bite-size fly in amber now rests beneath a slumbering black bear.

She finds delectable bite-size hacks to tolerate the Shaconage of life in a two-hundred square foot walk-up three-thousand miles from her children. *Drastic times require drastic measures. Breadwinners are sometimes bi-coastal.* Something like that.

Maybe it's *Have more earning potential than your husband and find yourself commuting 3,560 miles where you wake up before dawn to Facetime the fifteen-year-old who hates you for leaving but still needs help with an essay on* Lord of the Flies *due before she leaves for a soccer retreat.*

They become Golding's British boys; one stranded on an island called Pico-Robertson; one, Hunters Cove; each disastrously unable to govern herself. Flights home every five or six weeks are an exercise in Bermuda Triangle physics. She disappears and reappears with no one the wiser.

The blur between reality and fiction a mystic zipper in the body bag of her long-distance parenting. Is she the family's hero or just another Ursus americanus hibernating in a hollow log on the opposite coast? The treason of parenting.

Twelve seasons of twenty-two episodes each, *Murder, She Wrote* plays a continuous loop when she isn't at work or failing to connect with her kids. Her bucket list includes a stay at the Blair House Inn, Mendocino: *A mystery lover's dream.* J.B. Fletcher's fictional house in the fictional town of Cabot Cove where fictional murders are solved, and no one must leave their family. The population remains 3,560.

In episode six of season one, "Hit, Run, and Homicide," Jessica is captured inside a remote-control car speeding toward the edge of a faux Maine sea cliff. She bangs her fists on the driver-side window wanting to get out. It's all moving too fast.

Summer with Its Humidity

and I don't brush my wet hair
allowing it to tussle into a clematis wreath,
the kind Margaret Fuller handwove
on the banks of the Concord while pausing
mid-German translations for the day.

A sudden quiet like loose tendrils
from my front porch view of our little oak
whose stretch of limbs boasts his spring growth.
Tilting right, one branch boldly askew

like nature's own young Werther:
"What did you expect me to do, you who
planted then abandoned, coming home June
and July expecting only a crisp edge

in the breeze?" And so the oak too greets
my return with church pews of distance.
A bicoastal pace I cannot keep but do. Older,
my children a riot of cabbage and ferns. Fuller

knew "the only object in life is to grow."
Moisture disrupts the bonds of hair. Is this where
I'm not enough? Where mothers working
months from home sink into river mud? Meet

the frizz of distance. Yet Fuller too was
underestimated. I unfurl a picnic for cabbage
and ferns. Pin damp hair to an imaginary
bonnet, let humidity weave us wild.

Plastic Orange Lei

Alone in August with my boy. Waist
level to the bend of our knees' semi-
fetal postures in a Tiguan VW womb.
It holds mother and son while steeling
the faux-festive glow of Dollar Tree
flowers on a string. My son's effort
to fit in. His first day of twelfth grade
and the plastic orange lei wears him.
He is sad. Lifts both hands to summer
curls and vents the morning's mishap.
WSA's senior car parade fell flat,
no cheering underclassmen. He drove

alone, only to be separated en route.
Why didn't anyone wait? For him
air thickens, fists contract. Laboring
smooth, second-born and easiest. One
year of high school left and his face
wears the rust of disappointment.
My buddy this golden butterfly hero
rush of good energy and optimism
has worn leis twice before. At five
he wanted to match the blossoms,
orange king zinnias and Japanese
camellias at the Huntington Museum
Children's Garden. In third grade
he hulaed to ukuleles for a class Luau.
Over his head and flung to the trunk
slack, this third lei has lost its charm.
Now he is crying on my shoulder:

I refuse to let it define my senior year.
Sometimes all a mother can offer
is space and food. I pull my breakfast
orange from the dashboard, half-peeled.
We sit like a Dutch still life. Private
study in pulp, we shred the sour rind.
How I wanted my mother's affection,
the way she loved her sons. Floral
bright how I love my wounded boy.
Our hearts easily split. We are encased
in the suffering of those we cherish,
transform behind metal and glass.

The Death of Lowly Worm

People have no problem being cruel.
Find a dying rattle snake
On the side of the road in the Angeles National Forest?
Google if you can eat it. How to
Skin it. Dare your twelve-year-old daughter

To make the first cut.
And now your daughter is my client.

We work on a draft of her college essay,
Her desire to study biomedical engineering at UCLA.
What if I demonstrate my interest in animals?
Compassion if you can tolerate it. How she
Butchered it. Told me not to worry;

It tasted like chicken.
We needed a hook to catch their attention.
And I am hooked in the throat

Like a bass or a pike or trout in Lake Isabella.
Cincinnati and I'm twenty-one again
Ready for the law firm picnic. Just an intern, am I in love?
He's a law student telling me what to file;
I'm in the fax room in heels.

I miss the bus and call my brother to pick me up
At the nearest station northwest
Of the city. *You'll learn the system,* he tells me.
It's different from making tuna subs at Subway, huh?
When the law student meets him

He doesn't shake his hand. Cruelty keeps us
From each other. They make fun of his name

And explain he's not up to snuff.
Don't you know you can do better, Candice?
And I don't want to do better
But learn life is nothing like Richard Scarry
Told us. Rattle snakes skinned, eaten by a little girl.

Ludicrous Optimism Pantoum

I cannot look away from the bald eagles
Jackie and Shadow and their three eggs
Atop some tree where they've built a nest
Of sticks and grass and stalks and sod

Jackie and Shadow and their three eggs
Performing live for the Big Bear Valley
with sticks and grass and stalks and sod
I cannot resist a bit of ludicrous optimism

Performing live for the Big Bear Valley
Cameras feeding thousands of watchers
Hungry for a taste of ludicrous optimism
Rather than some Biden-Trump rematch

YouTube feeds thousands of watchers
Suggested videos like the *Daily Show*
Clip tackling the Biden-Trump rematch
When all we need is Jackie and Shadow

Instead of shitty ads for Jon Stewart
Or the call from my son who's hit a deer
And I cry thinking of Jackie's dedication
The sixty-two hours protecting her clutch

I call to comfort my son about the deer
As he waits in the cold and dark and wind
Six hours for a truck to clutch and tow
The crumpled steel from a Georgia ditch

Jackie waits in the cold and dark and wind
For Shadow to deliver a fish or a big stick
She pipes a whistle of high-pitched approval
Joins the rest of us in ludicrous optimism

Ode to a Bartender at the Charlotte Douglas Airport, Terminal A

I

Her pink-accent shock-blond bob
and sad-face emoji tattoo soften
the sting of not asking for my ID,
the before-noon margarita drinker

in me. Her library copy of *It* atop
the Avantco refrigerator, a badly
tattered Stephen King near her
sweating, half-drunk strawberry

lemonade from Burger King
distracts me from the intensifying
pro-Palestinian protests and arrests
at UCLA and Columbia on the TV,

from the humanitarian crisis in Gaza,
from the failed cease fire and dead
hostages. Today's school shooting.
I ask her what it's like tending to us.

II

She shares her customer journal, fir
leather record of human wilderness,
a bookmark ribbon like a picket line
she boldly crosses. Firing questions at

her daily patrons. I open and read:
If you could give your childhood self
advice today, what would it be? Chris
writes, *Hey kid, life will throw you*

*curveballs—remember the sun shines
brightest in the darkness.* Beside, *I hate
my job,* Clint confesses—*my fiancé
recently decided we should now go*

our separate ways. "Just G" admits,
I'm not bulletproof, no one fucking is.
On one page is Mick—*I hate clowns.*
Is life a pattern of connecting flights?

III

How I'm falling for this barmaid
who asks me to contribute, taps her pen.
She can tackle an 1100-page novel,
serve tequila lemon drop martinis and

raspberry Schnapps, offer Casamigos
to the lonely and bored, the judgmental
and despairing, all of us hurting who
find ease in forgetting, in discussing

single-barrel bourbon instead. We
wait for layover flights and peace
this first day of September at CLT
where the Supremes chirp *Baby Love*.

Pouring my margarita, salting the rim
with curiosity, she asks what I yearn for.
To finish this stanza before I board,
I lie. Then softening, admit it's *hope*.

Menopause: A Cento from Female Poets Laureate

She has a secret humble wish[1]
to practice yoga, take piano lessons,
rewrite her drama rife with lust and pride.[2]

Try it: all you'll get is pieces—the sun
emerging from behind the mountain ridge,
smoke coming off the ice on a thawing lake.[3]

I was a thought, a dream, a fish, a wing
And then a human being
When I emerged from my mother's river.[4]

Surely spring has been returned to me, this time
not as a lover but a messenger of death, yet
it is still spring, it is still meant tenderly.[5]

---

[1] "The Ugly Old Lady," Josephine Jacobsen
[2] "The Revisionist Dream," Maxine Kumin
[3] "Voiceover," Rita Dove
[4] "Granddaughters," Joy Harjo
[5] "Vita Nova," Louise Gluck

I mark the pages of a mail-order catalog,
listen for passing cars. All day we watch
for the mail, some news from a distant place.[6]

Then animals long believed gone crept down
From trees. We took new stock of one another.
We wept to be reminded of such color.[7]

All these great barns out here in the outskirts,
black creosote boards knee-deep in the bluegrass.
They look so beautifully abandoned, even in use.[8]

---

[6] "Housekeeping," Natasha Trethewey
[7] "An Old Story," Tracy K. Smith
[8] "What It Looks Like to Us and the Words We Use," Ada Limón

Ghazal Where I Learn to Love Myself

My lover's eyes sing patterns of rhyme,
but for me it's those lips.

Fleshy enjambment where I end-stop,
the perfect couplet, those lips.

Pressed together like Charon's obol,
if my death could be so blessed.

A modern libation poured for Aphrodite,
both poetry and prose lips.

My lover's smile is mine, sharp as scimitar,
sliced top from bottom—

Parting ways we flash a pearly shift,
glossy-toothed *kameez.* Oh lips!

My own mouth my muse, I tongue
an invocation, call for inspiration:

Passion's incarnation, my lover is me.
Resurrecting save-my-soul lips.

Like the fifth *bayt* in an ancient *ghazal*,
they round in rhyme-refrain.

A closing of flesh and pucker of hush,
I marvel at broke-my-mold lips.

Not to whistle but to kiss, my own
tender embrace I no longer resist.

Whispering *Candice,* I touch my ear
and hear self-love with these lips.

May Day, May Day

I watch airline disaster documentaries
the day after the 2024 presidential election
while my optimism hits the California countryside
while my hope nosedives into the Pacific
while my joy spirals into the Peruvian jungle
while all possibility is shot down by a Russian missile
because the four chambers of my heart stall
and I attempt to glide to a smooth landing
but my landing gear won't lower
but my instruments aren't working
but my windshield has been shattered
so I tell every attendant version of myself
to tell every frightened passenger I have ever been
to brace for an emergency landing
and I adjust the flaps pretending they will slow
reality from slamming into the next four years
happy to know the cockpit voice recorder
will document just how badly we needed help

Chimneys and Buddhas

A state of emergency remains
In Los Angeles County
Red flag warnings and reigning

Evacuation orders choke like smoke
As the Santa Anas continue
To float the flames and chaos

Like political firebrands
Blaming our governor and reopening
Trump's feud like a wound

But fires have no loyalty
And cross canyons like aisles
Because piles of ash aren't partisan

I think of my twelfth-grade students
Who just returned to L.A.
From visiting the ruins of Auschwitz

Arm in arm they sang *Sh'ma*
Young Jewish voices a cosmic waterdrop
With guitars inside crematoriums

How Altadena and the Palisades prove
Life's irony—often the only
Things left standing are the chimneys

But today I see footage of the Malibu
Feed Bin burned at PCH
And Topanga where some things remain

Five smiling granite Buddhas
Ancient sentinel survivors offering
Our eyes a pool of soft hope

Fist Pump

A golden shovel after Ellen Bass' "Kiss"

As fires pummeled, his Pomeranian was heartache floating
lost and alone in the rubble by a pool.
Colvin didn't hesitate. He knew he wasn't
at the end. Oreo was his baby
to rescue, his heart racing, and a palm
within reach. Wanting Oreo's fragile breast,
a lifeline of L.A.'s scream. An unanswered need
in his arms, safe and quick, quicker.
Shiny as flames, entering the Palisades, he felt it.
Broadcast by NBC's Liz K, with mic and Doc Martens,
renewing all hope for Oreo. His radiant face
trotted toward the gate, Colvin's palm to jaw,
reaching awkwardly, all love and thumbs.
On video, the wailing of his lungs,
tousled with smoke. Joy comes like water
pumping from above. Like one lizard
more or less, a dog is a life
who matters. He scooped Oreo up until
he couldn't hold back.
Like a toddler to his shoulder, hot breath
in plumes, Colvin fist pumped high over ashen cement.
The rescue went viral; a wagging tail darted off.

This Tender Dwelling

is an open floor plan—
of upper & lower chambers.
My two-story heart
an arrhythmic aesthetic of curb appeal
nestled in the cul-de-sac

of me. Living,
an attempt at hospitality.
But vinyl siding peels from sun & storms.
Until the interior succumbs
years of wear & tear.

Funny phrase *wear & tear*
for fifty years of feet
crossing thresholds:

muddy ones
loud ones
reckless & careless words
spilled by vandals of the heart.
Stains appear
on new carpet. Silliness,

preparing softness like soil,
calendula & verbena
in full sun. Dream
of ghost blooms
bringing worth to the square footage

of me. Have you loved
yourself? Cleaned
the furnace filters & vacuumed
HVAC diffuser vents? Have you
tested the smoke alarms
in the most private rooms of your heart?

Or have you too
with a sledgehammer
feathered drywall,
letting the vicious world ravage your
earnest pipes? Even so,
keep clean gratitude for small things,
don't we—
where stents repair
arterial walls,
like sage sticks smudge sacred
spaces & open
iambic paths

for green fists that beat toward
a humble & silky life.
Our bones, built to enter
& exit, we can excite
love even after pipes freeze,
expand & crack.

What's the deductible for heartbreak?

Today I ask my son
to visit the college he will attend,
his new home come fall.
It's January 20th & who can call
this country

home? The window of a local shop
in some tiny Georgia town
displays Christian tea towels & other tchotchkes.
My wide-eyed boy doesn't notice:

its T-shirt of *10 Reasons*
Men prefer Guns over Women.

I've always imagined
hospitality could transcend human nature.
Our need to destroy
open & tender offerings
can be righted by peonies. Love
is the cul-de-sac of returns,
a child's future.

Fine, Mary Oliver. I will
unroll the WELCOME mat & offer entrance
the way my son will.
What beauty can we find,
tearing up the carpet, enjoying
this morning's dew
with you,
or anyone else who knocks?

About the Author

Candice M. Kelsey is a writer and educator living in both Los Angeles and Georgia.

She is the author of seven books: *Generation MySpace: Helping Your Teen Survive Online Adolescence* (Marlowe & Co., 2007), *Still I am Pushing* (Finishing Line Press, 2020), *A ~~Girl / Woman / Teacher /~~ Poet* (Alien Buddha Press, 2022), *The Poet Dreams of Driving a Ding-A-Ling Ice Cream Truck* (Pine Row Press, 2023), *Puzzling Things: Essays* (Fauxmoir Press, 2023), *Choose Your Own Poem* (Cherry Dress Press, 2023), and *Postcards from the Masthead* (boats against the current press, 2024).

Longlisted by *Wigleaf's* Top 50 Short Fiction in 2024 and a finalist for a Best Microfiction 2023, she won the University of Cincinnati Library's Books by the Banks Prize 2022 and the Rebecca Laird Poetry Prize 2020. Her work has been featured in *SWWIM, The Laurel Review, Poet Lore, Passengers Journal,* and *About Place,* among others. She reads for *The Los Angeles Review* and is an unabashed fangirl of all things *Murder, She Wrote,* opera, and the Los Angeles Dodgers.

Website: www.candicemkelseypoet.com
Socials: @Feed_Me_Poetry

www.ingramcontent.com/pod-product-compliance
Lightning Source LLC
Chambersburg PA
CBHW022012160426
43197CB00007B/400